Caesar Salad Dressing

Elevate Your Salads with Delicious Homemade Dressings

While every precaution has been taken in the preparation of this book, the publisher assumes no responsibility for errors or omissions, or for damages resulting from the use of the information contained herein.

CAESAR SALAD DRESSING

First edition. October 27, 2023.

Copyright © 2023 john ahmad.

ISBN: 979-8223969990

Written by john ahmad.

Table of Contents

John Ahmad

Chapter 1: Classic Caesar Salad Dressing

Welcome to the world of Caesar salad dressings, where flavors mingle, textures dance, and a rich culinary heritage unfolds. In this cookbook, we embark on a journey through the tantalizing universe of Caesar salad dressings, from its intriguing origins to the contemporary reinventions that grace our modern tables.

Traditional Caesar Dressing: A Timeless Recipe

The origins of Caesar salad dressing are steeped in history, tracing back to the ingenious culinary mind of Caesar Cardini in the 1920s. In this chapter, we pay homage to the traditional and authentic Caesar dressing that started it all. We'll break down the classic recipe into its fundamental components, guiding you through each step to ensure you create a dressing that captures the essence of its original form.

Ingredients:

- 2 garlic cloves, minced
- 2 anchovy fillets (or anchovy paste), finely chopped
- 1 teaspoon Dijon mustard
- 1 tablespoon freshly squeezed lemon juice
- 1 large egg yolk, preferably pasteurized
- 1/2 cup extra-virgin olive oil
- 1/4 cup grated Parmesan cheese
- Salt and freshly ground black pepper, to taste

Instructions:

1. In a mixing bowl, combine the minced garlic and chopped anchovy

fillets, mashing them together with the back of a spoon until a paste-like consistency forms.

2. Add the Dijon mustard and lemon juice to the bowl, whisking the mixture until well combined.
3. Gently whisk in the egg yolk, ensuring it is thoroughly incorporated into the dressing.
4. While continuously whisking, slowly drizzle in the olive oil in a steady stream until the dressing emulsifies and thickens.
5. Stir in the grated Parmesan cheese and season with salt and pepper to taste, adjusting the seasoning to suit your preference.

Pro Tips:

1. For a creamier texture, add a dollop of mayonnaise or Greek yogurt to the dressing.
2. If you prefer a smoother dressing, blend all the ingredients together in a food processor or blender.
3. Adjust the tanginess of the dressing by varying the amount of lemon juice or vinegar used.

Adding a Twist: Creative Variations of the Classic

While the traditional Caesar dressing holds a cherished place in our hearts, sometimes it's thrilling to infuse new life into a beloved classic. In this section, we encourage you to let your culinary creativity shine as we explore an array of creative variations on the classic Caesar dressing.

Savory Herb Caesar Dressing:

Elevate the classic dressing with an assortment of fresh herbs like basil, parsley, or tarragon, adding a burst of aromatic flavors to your salad.

Roasted Garlic Caesar Dressing:

Embrace the sweet and mellow taste of roasted garlic, which lends a deeper complexity to the dressing, making each bite a delight.

Citrus-Kissed Caesar Dressing:

Incorporate the zesty goodness of oranges, grapefruits, or mandarins to create a bright and refreshing dressing with a citrusy twist.

Blue Cheese Caesar Dressing:

For blue cheese enthusiasts, blend the richness of blue cheese with the classic Caesar dressing, introducing a creamy and tangy fusion.

Smoky Bacon Caesar Dressing:

Indulge in the irresistible allure of smoky bacon, adding a savory dimension that pairs perfectly with the classic flavors.

Explore these variations and more, and let your imagination guide you as you embark on a flavor-filled journey. The possibilities are endless when it comes to reinventing the classic Caesar dressing, so don your chef's hat and embark on a dressing adventure like never before. Get ready to reimagine your salads and impress your guests with inventive twists on a timeless favorite.

Chapter 2: Creamy Avocado Caesar Dressing

Creamy Goodness: Avocado-Infused Twist

Avocado, nature's velvety gift, has taken the culinary world by storm, and for a good reason! In this chapter, we explore the magic of avocados and how they can transform the classic Caesar dressing into a creamy, dreamy delight. Whether you're an avocado aficionado or a newcomer to this green wonder, get ready to experience the lusciousness of avocado in every spoonful of this dressing.

Ingredients:

- 1 ripe avocado, peeled and pitted
- 2 tablespoons freshly squeezed lemon juice
- 2 cloves garlic, minced
- 1/4 cup extra-virgin olive oil
- 1 tablespoon Dijon mustard
- Salt and freshly ground black pepper, to taste

Instructions:

1. In a food processor or blender, combine the peeled and pitted avocado, lemon juice, and minced garlic.
2. Blend the ingredients until smooth and creamy, scraping down the sides of the processor or blender as needed.
3. Add the Dijon mustard and continue blending until well incorporated.
4. With the processor or blender running on low speed, drizzle in the olive oil gradually until the dressing emulsifies and reaches the desired consistency.
5. Season the dressing with salt and freshly ground black pepper, adjusting the seasoning to your taste preferences.

Pro Tips:

To make the dressing thinner, add a bit of water or vegetable broth while blending until you achieve the desired consistency.

Customize the creaminess by adjusting the amount of avocado used. For an intensely creamy dressing, add an extra avocado.

Vegan and Dairy-Free Options

Embracing a vegan or dairy-free lifestyle doesn't mean missing out on the delightful flavors of a Caesar salad dressing. In this section, we present you with simple and delicious alternatives, ensuring that everyone can enjoy the creamy goodness of a Caesar dressing without compromising their dietary choices.

Cashew Caesar Dressing:

Harness the richness of soaked and blended cashews to achieve a smooth and creamy texture that rivals traditional dairy-based dressings.

Tofu-Tahini Caesar Dressing:

Blend silken tofu with tahini to create a protein-packed, dairy-free dressing that boasts a luscious creaminess.

Coconut Cream Caesar Dressing:

Utilize the creamy goodness of coconut cream, combined with lemon juice and garlic, to achieve a tropical twist on the classic Caesar dressing.

Almond Milk-Based Caesar Dressing:

Blend unsweetened almond milk with garlic and Dijon mustard for a light and refreshing dressing that's perfect for drizzling over your favorite greens.

Whichever vegan or dairy-free option you choose, rest assured that your Caesar salad will be transformed into a luxurious and guilt-free indulgence. Let the avocado and vegan magic unfold, creating dressings that cater to a variety of palates and dietary needs. Get ready to savor the creaminess and depth of flavor without compromising on your lifestyle choices. It's time to experience the allure of avocado and the creative world of vegan and dairy-free Caesar dressings.

Chapter 3: Zesty Lemon and Garlic Dressing

Bright and Tangy: Lemony Freshness

In this chapter, we dive into the invigorating world of zesty lemon and explore how its vibrant flavor can elevate the classic Caesar dressing to new heights. The brightness of fresh lemon infuses the dressing with a refreshing tang that awakens the palate and complements a variety of salad greens. Join us as we celebrate the citrusy essence of lemons and create a dressing that breathes new life into your salads.

Ingredients:

- 1/4 cup freshly squeezed lemon juice
- 1 teaspoon lemon zest
- 2 garlic cloves, minced
- 1/2 cup extra-virgin olive oil
- 1 teaspoon honey (or maple syrup for a vegan option)
- Salt and freshly ground black pepper, to taste

Instructions:

1. In a mixing bowl, combine the freshly squeezed lemon juice, lemon zest, and minced garlic, stirring well to combine.
2. Slowly drizzle in the olive oil while continuously whisking the mixture, allowing the dressing to emulsify and thicken.
3. Stir in the honey (or maple syrup for a vegan alternative) to add a touch of sweetness that balances the tanginess of the lemon.
4. Season the dressing with salt and freshly ground black pepper, adjusting the flavors to your liking.

Pro Tips:

1. For a more pronounced lemon flavor, increase the amount of lemon zest used.

2. To achieve a smoother dressing, blend the ingredients together in a blender or food processor.

Balancing the Garlic Flavor

While garlic brings a savory and aromatic punch to the dressing, finding the right balance is key to ensuring it doesn't overpower the other flavors. In this section, we share tips on using garlic effectively in your lemon-infused Caesar dressing, ensuring it enhances the overall taste without overwhelming the palate.

Roasted Garlic Elegance:

Roasting garlic mellows its pungency and brings out a subtle sweetness. Add roasted garlic to your dressing for a milder yet flavorful garlic experience.

Infused Garlic Oil:

Prepare garlic-infused oil by heating olive oil with garlic cloves until fragrant. Strain the oil and use it as the base for your dressing to impart a gentle garlic essence.

Adjustable Garlic Intensity:

Start with a smaller amount of minced garlic and gradually increase it according to your taste preferences. Allow the dressing to sit for a few minutes to let the flavors meld before adjusting further.

Balancing the lemony freshness with the right amount of garlic creates a harmonious dressing that invigorates your taste buds with every bite. Explore these techniques and savor the bright and tangy allure of lemon as it blends seamlessly with the enchanting essence of garlic. Get ready to dress your salads with zesty sophistication and culinary finesse.

Chapter 4: Anchovy Lovers' Delight

Embracing Umami: The Role of Anchovies

Anchovies, those tiny and often misunderstood fish, hold the secret to unlocking a world of umami richness in your Caesar dressing. In this chapter, we explore the umami powerhouse that is the anchovy and how it imparts a depth of flavor that truly elevates the dressing. Whether you're already an anchovy enthusiast or curious to explore their culinary potential, this dressing is sure to delight your taste buds.

Ingredients:

- 4-5 anchovy fillets (or 1-2 teaspoons anchovy paste)
- 2 garlic cloves, minced
- 1 tablespoon Dijon mustard
- 1/4 cup freshly squeezed lemon juice
- 1/2 cup extra-virgin olive oil
- 1/4 cup grated Parmesan cheese
- Salt and freshly ground black pepper, to taste

Instructions:

1. In a mixing bowl, mash the anchovy fillets (or anchovy paste) together with the minced garlic to create a flavorful paste.
2. Add the Dijon mustard and freshly squeezed lemon juice to the bowl, whisking the mixture until well combined.
3. Gradually drizzle in the olive oil while continuously whisking, allowing the dressing to emulsify and achieve a smooth consistency.
4. Stir in the grated Parmesan cheese, incorporating it into the dressing for added creaminess.
5. Season the dressing with salt and freshly ground black pepper, adjusting the flavors to your liking.

Pro Tips:

1. If using whole anchovy fillets, make sure to chop them finely or use a mortar and pestle to create a paste.
2. Anchovy paste is a convenient alternative and can be found in tubes or small jars at most grocery stores.

Alternatives for Anchovy Haters

Not everyone is keen on the distinctive taste of anchovies, and that's perfectly fine! This section caters to those who prefer to skip the anchovy flavor while still enjoying the essence of a Caesar dressing. We've got you covered with a couple of delicious alternatives that ensure your dressing remains flavorful and satisfying.

Soy Sauce Savvy:

Incorporate a touch of soy sauce into your dressing to infuse the umami goodness without the anchovy flavor. It's an excellent alternative for those who enjoy a savory kick.

Miso Magic:

Miso paste brings a delightful balance of saltiness and umami, elevating your dressing with its complex flavor. Experiment with light or dark miso to find your preferred intensity.

By embracing these anchovy alternatives, you can create a dressing that resonates with your taste preferences while preserving the umami charm. Discover the joy of umami-rich dressings without a hint of anchovy, making it an appealing option for all Caesar salad enthusiasts. Prepare to savor the delightful balance of flavors that this dressing has to offer, regardless of your anchovy inclinations.

Chapter 5: Spicy Caesar Dressing

Kick it Up: Adding Some Heat

In this chapter, we turn up the heat and dive into the world of spicy Caesar dressings. For those who crave a bit of fiery excitement in their salads, this dressing is sure to ignite your taste buds with its delightful kick. We explore various ways to infuse heat into the classic Caesar dressing, creating a zesty and invigorating flavor profile that's perfect for those who love a little spice in their lives.

Ingredients:

- 2 garlic cloves, minced
- 1-2 teaspoons hot sauce (adjust to your preferred spice level)
- 1 tablespoon Dijon mustard
- 1/4 cup freshly squeezed lemon juice
- 1/2 cup extra-virgin olive oil
- 1 teaspoon red pepper flakes (adjust to taste)
- Salt and freshly ground black pepper, to taste

Instructions:

1. In a mixing bowl, combine the minced garlic, hot sauce, and Dijon mustard, mixing well to ensure the spices are evenly distributed.
2. Add the freshly squeezed lemon juice to the bowl, whisking the mixture until the flavors meld together.
3. Gradually drizzle in the olive oil while continuously whisking, allowing the dressing to emulsify and achieve a creamy consistency.
4. Sprinkle in the red pepper flakes, adjusting the amount to suit your desired level of spiciness.
5. Season the dressing with salt and freshly ground black pepper, tasting as you go to ensure the spice level is just right.

Pro Tips:

1. Experiment with different types of hot sauce to find one that complements your taste preferences. Whether you prefer a smoky chipotle kick or a fiery habanero punch, the choice is yours.
2. For an extra spicy twist, add a dash of cayenne pepper or a finely chopped chili pepper to the dressing.

Customizing the Spice Level

The beauty of making your own spicy Caesar dressing lies in the ability to customize the spice level according to your unique palate. In this section, we guide you through adjusting the heat to suit your taste buds, ensuring your dressing strikes the perfect balance between tangy, creamy, and spicy.

Mild Heat Marvel:

If you're new to spicy dressings, start with a smaller amount of hot sauce and red pepper flakes. Gradually increase the spice level until you find your preferred mild heat.

Medium Spice Sensation:

For those who enjoy a bit of kick but don't want it too overpowering, opt for a moderate amount of hot sauce and red pepper flakes, striking a pleasant balance between tanginess and spice.

Fiery Flavor Feast:

Heat enthusiasts can go all out by adding generous amounts of hot sauce and red pepper flakes, resulting in a dressing that packs a serious punch.

By customizing the spice level, you have the power to create a spicy Caesar dressing that perfectly matches your taste preferences. Whether you prefer a gentle warmth or a fiery explosion of flavor, get ready to ignite your salads with a dressing that adds an exciting and vibrant twist to your culinary repertoire. Embrace the boldness of spice and enjoy the delightful journey of a spicy Caesar dressing that tantalizes your taste buds with every bite.

Chapter 6: Mediterranean Caesar Dressing

Mediterranean Flair: Olives, Feta, and More

In this chapter, we take a culinary trip to the sun-kissed Mediterranean shores and infuse the classic Caesar dressing with the bold and vibrant flavors of the region. Embrace the allure of olives, tangy feta cheese, and other Mediterranean delights as they harmonize with the familiar Caesar dressing, creating a fusion of tastes that will transport your taste buds to the coastal landscapes of Greece and Italy.

Ingredients:

- 1/4 cup pitted Kalamata olives, finely chopped
- 1/4 cup crumbled feta cheese
- 1 tablespoon freshly squeezed lemon juice
- 1 garlic clove, minced
- 1/2 cup extra-virgin olive oil
- 1 teaspoon Dijon mustard
- 1/2 teaspoon dried oregano
- Salt and freshly ground black pepper, to taste

Instructions:

1. In a mixing bowl, combine the chopped Kalamata olives, crumbled feta cheese, freshly squeezed lemon juice, and minced garlic, tossing the ingredients together to evenly distribute the flavors.
2. Add the Dijon mustard and dried oregano to the bowl, whisking the mixture until the ingredients meld into a Mediterranean-infused harmony.
3. Gradually drizzle in the olive oil while continuously whisking, allowing the dressing to emulsify and achieve a creamy consistency.
4. Season the dressing with salt and freshly ground black pepper, adjusting the flavors to your liking.

Pro Tips:

1. For an extra burst of Mediterranean flavors, toss in some chopped sun-dried tomatoes, artichoke hearts, or capers.
2. If you prefer a creamier texture, blend the dressing ingredients together in a blender or food processor.

Exploring Mediterranean Herbs

The Mediterranean region is a treasure trove of herbs, each boasting distinctive fragrances and flavors that enhance the Caesar dressing in unique ways. In this section, we invite you to explore the enchanting world of Mediterranean herbs and discover how they elevate the dressing to a new level of culinary splendor.

Basil Brilliance:

Embrace the aromatic charm of fresh basil, adding a delightful sweet and peppery note to the dressing that pairs beautifully with olives and feta.

Thyme Time:

Introduce dried or fresh thyme to the dressing for a subtle earthy flavor that complements the tanginess of the lemon and olives.

Rosemary Reverie:

Experience the woody and piney essence of rosemary, which adds a touch of Mediterranean elegance to your Caesar dressing.

Mint Magic:

Enliven your dressing with a refreshing burst of mint, imparting a bright and cooling sensation that harmonizes with the other Mediterranean flavors.

Indulge in the diverse array of Mediterranean herbs to create a Caesar dressing that transports your senses to the Mediterranean coast. The fusion of olives, feta, and these enchanting herbs will awaken your taste buds to the timeless allure of Mediterranean cuisine. Prepare to savor the richness of flavors that this dressing offers, as it transforms your salads into a vibrant and mouthwatering Mediterranean feast.

Chapter 7: Light and Healthy Yogurt-Based Dressing

Lightening Up: Using Yogurt as a Base

In this chapter, we delve deeper into the art of crafting a light and healthy Caesar dressing by embracing yogurt as the star ingredient. Yogurt not only contributes to a creamy and velvety texture but also infuses the dressing with a refreshing tang that harmonizes beautifully with the other flavors. Whether you're seeking a lighter alternative or simply appreciate the delightful taste of yogurt, this dressing will transform your salads into a guilt-free indulgence.

Ingredients:

- 1/2 cup plain Greek yogurt
- 1 tablespoon freshly squeezed lemon juice
- 1 garlic clove, minced
- 1 tablespoon Dijon mustard
- 1/4 cup extra-virgin olive oil
- 1 tablespoon grated Parmesan cheese
- 1 teaspoon honey (optional, for a touch of sweetness)
- Salt and freshly ground black pepper, to taste

Instructions:

1. In a mixing bowl, combine the plain Greek yogurt, freshly squeezed lemon juice, and minced garlic, stirring well to create a creamy and tangy yogurt base.
2. Add the Dijon mustard to the bowl, whisking the mixture until the flavors meld together harmoniously.
3. Gradually drizzle in the olive oil while continuously whisking, allowing the dressing to emulsify and achieve a smooth and velvety consistency.
4. Stir in the grated Parmesan cheese, which adds a subtle richness to the

dressing without overwhelming it with heaviness.

5. For a touch of sweetness, incorporate honey and continue whisking until it's well distributed throughout the dressing.

6. Season the dressing with a pinch of salt and freshly ground black pepper, fine-tuning the flavors to your desired balance.

Pro Tips:

1. To make this dressing completely vegan, simply omit the Parmesan cheese and use maple syrup instead of honey.

2. Feel free to adjust the lemon juice quantity to your preference, depending on how tangy you want the dressing to be.

Flavorful Herbs and Seasonings

While yogurt forms the creamy foundation, it's the addition of flavorful herbs and seasonings that truly elevates this dressing to a new level of culinary delight. In this section, we explore an array of herbs and spices that complement the yogurt base, resulting in a dressing that is both refreshingly tangy and rich in savory goodness.

Chive Charm:

Introduce the subtle onion-like flavor of fresh chives, adding a delicate touch of herbal brightness to the dressing that plays beautifully with the tanginess of the yogurt.

Parsley Perfection:

Incorporate the fresh and grassy essence of parsley, which not only enhances the dressing's visual appeal but also complements the other elements of a classic Caesar dressing.

Dill Delight:

Experience the refreshing flavor of dill, which infuses the dressing with a zesty and citrusy note that awakens the palate with each bite.

Cracked Black Pepper Finesse:

Enhance the dressing's savory character with a generous sprinkle of cracked black pepper, adding a touch of spiciness that harmonizes brilliantly with the tangy yogurt base.

By embracing the versatility of yogurt as a base and exploring the vibrant palette of herbs and seasonings, you'll create a light and healthy Caesar dressing that tantalizes your taste buds while nourishing your body. Savor the delightful balance of flavors, as the dressing transforms your salads into a delicious and guilt-free feast. Let the goodness of yogurt and the magic of Mediterranean-inspired seasonings transport you to a world of refreshing and wholesome taste sensations. Prepare to indulge in a light and healthy Caesar dressing that will become a staple in your salad repertoire.

Chapter 8: Caesar Vinaigrette

The Marriage of Vinaigrette and Caesar

In this chapter, we celebrate the union of two culinary powerhouses—the tangy vinaigrette and the beloved Caesar dressing. Together, they create a harmonious fusion known as the Caesar vinaigrette—a dressing that encapsulates the best of both worlds. Prepare to embark on a flavor journey that combines the brightness of vinaigrette with the richness of Caesar, resulting in a dressing that strikes a delightful balance on your palate.

Ingredients:

- 2 garlic cloves, minced
- 1 tablespoon Dijon mustard
- 1/4 cup freshly squeezed lemon juice
- 1 tablespoon Worcestershire sauce (optional, but adds depth of flavor)
- 1/2 cup extra-virgin olive oil
- 1/4 cup grated Parmesan cheese
- Salt and freshly ground black pepper, to taste

Instructions:

1. In a mixing bowl, combine the minced garlic and Dijon mustard, whisking them together to form a smooth and flavorful base.
2. Add the freshly squeezed lemon juice and Worcestershire sauce (if using) to the bowl, continuing to whisk the mixture until the flavors meld seamlessly.
3. Gradually drizzle in the olive oil while continuously whisking, allowing the vinaigrette to emulsify and achieve a balanced consistency.
4. Stir in the grated Parmesan cheese, which contributes a velvety richness to the dressing and enhances its depth of flavor.
5. Season the dressing with salt and freshly ground black pepper, adjusting the flavors to your liking.

Pro Tips:

1. If you prefer a creamier texture, blend the ingredients together in a blender or food processor until smooth.
2. Play with the amount of Worcestershire sauce to suit your taste—its umami essence adds a touch of complexity to the dressing.

Finding the Perfect Balance

Creating a Caesar vinaigrette is all about finding the sweet spot where the tangy brightness of vinaigrette meets the creamy richness of Caesar. In this section, we share tips on striking that perfect balance, ensuring that each ingredient complements the other to perfection.

Citrus Sensation:

Adjust the amount of lemon juice to achieve your desired level of tanginess. For a more pronounced citrus sensation, add a bit more lemon juice; for a milder tang, use less.

Mustard Magic:

Dijon mustard serves as the binding agent, infusing the dressing with a subtle spiciness. Fine-tune the amount of mustard to enhance the overall flavor without overpowering.

Cheesy Indulgence:

The grated Parmesan cheese adds a luxurious creaminess and a delightful umami touch. Strike the perfect balance by ensuring it enriches the dressing without becoming overly dominant.

Oil and Emulsification:

Gradually drizzle in the olive oil while whisking continuously, allowing the dressing to emulsify and create a smooth and velvety texture.

By mastering the art of balance, you'll create a Caesar vinaigrette that brings the best of both vinaigrette and Caesar dressing to your salads. Embrace the delightful harmony of flavors that this dressing offers, striking a beautiful symphony on your taste buds with each drizzle. Prepare to elevate your salads with a Caesar vinaigrette that marries two culinary worlds into a dressing that is truly exceptional.

Chapter 9: Bold and Smoky Chipotle Caesar Dressing

Smoky Sensation: Chipotle's Impact

In this chapter, we explore the bold and captivating flavors of chipotle and how they can transform the classic Caesar dressing into a smoky sensation that ignites the taste buds. Chipotle peppers, with their distinct smokiness and mild heat, add a delightful twist to the dressing, giving it a unique character that will leave you craving more. Get ready to embark on a culinary adventure that embraces the allure of chipotle and elevates your Caesar dressing to new heights of smoky deliciousness.

Ingredients:

- 1-2 chipotle peppers in adobo sauce (adjust to your desired heat level)
- 2 garlic cloves, minced
- 1 tablespoon Dijon mustard
- 1/4 cup freshly squeezed lemon juice
- 1/2 cup extra-virgin olive oil
- 1/4 cup grated Parmesan cheese
- Salt and freshly ground black pepper, to taste

Instructions:

1. In a food processor or blender, combine the chipotle peppers in adobo sauce and the minced garlic, blending until they form a smoky and flavorful paste.
2. Add the Dijon mustard and freshly squeezed lemon juice to the processor or blender, continuing to blend until the flavors are well incorporated.
3. Gradually pour in the olive oil in a steady stream while the processor or blender is running on low speed, allowing the dressing to emulsify and achieve a creamy texture.

4. Stir in the grated Parmesan cheese, infusing the dressing with a velvety richness that balances the smokiness of the chipotle.
5. Season the dressing with salt and freshly ground black pepper, adjusting the flavors to your liking.

Pro Tips:

1. To control the heat level, start by adding one chipotle pepper to the blender. Taste the dressing, and if you desire more heat, add another pepper accordingly.
2. You can find canned chipotle peppers in adobo sauce at most grocery stores.

Adjusting the Heat

The allure of chipotle lies not only in its smoky flavor but also in its heat. In this section, we explore ways to adjust the spiciness of the dressing, ensuring it matches your preference for mild warmth or fiery intensity.

Mild and Smoky:

If you prefer a gentle kick, use just one chipotle pepper or use a smaller amount of adobo sauce to temper the heat.

Balanced Heat Burst:

Embrace the perfect balance of smokiness and heat by using one to two chipotle peppers, depending on your tolerance for spiciness.

Fiery Flavor Fiesta:

For those who revel in fiery sensations, add additional chipotle peppers or a bit more adobo sauce to create a dressing that packs a serious punch.

By adjusting the heat to your liking, you'll create a bold and smoky Caesar dressing that tantalizes your taste buds with each bite. Embrace the captivating flavors of chipotle and let its smoky essence transform your salads into a culinary masterpiece. Prepare to savor the delightful harmony of flavors as the dressing adds a smoky sensation that sets your Caesar salad apart from the rest. Get ready for a smoky adventure that elevates your Caesar dressing to a whole new level of excitement.

Chapter 10: Roasted Garlic and Parmesan Dressing

Rich and Robust: Roasting Garlic for Depth

In this chapter, we delve into the enchanting world of roasted garlic and how it elevates the classic Caesar dressing to a rich and robust masterpiece. Roasting garlic imparts a mellow and caramelized flavor that enhances the dressing's depth, creating a luxurious experience for your taste buds. Join us as we unlock the secrets of roasting garlic to perfection and infuse it into the dressing for an extraordinary culinary delight.

Ingredients:

- 1 whole head of garlic
- 1 tablespoon olive oil
- 1 tablespoon Dijon mustard
- 1/4 cup freshly squeezed lemon juice
- 1/2 cup extra-virgin olive oil
- 1/4 cup grated Parmesan cheese
- Salt and freshly ground black pepper, to taste

Instructions:

1. Preheat your oven to 400°F (200°C).
2. Slice off the top of the whole head of garlic to expose the cloves.
3. Place the garlic head on a piece of aluminum foil, drizzle with olive oil, and wrap it tightly in the foil.
4. Roast the garlic in the preheated oven for approximately 40-45 minutes, or until the cloves are soft and golden brown.
5. Once roasted, let the garlic cool slightly, then squeeze the soft, caramelized cloves into a mixing bowl.
6. Add the Dijon mustard and freshly squeezed lemon juice to the bowl, whisking them together with the roasted garlic to form a smooth and

flavorful base.

7. Gradually drizzle in the extra-virgin olive oil while whisking continuously, allowing the dressing to emulsify and achieve a velvety texture.
8. Stir in the grated Parmesan cheese, which enhances the dressing with a savory richness that complements the roasted garlic.
9. Season the dressing with salt and freshly ground black pepper, adjusting the flavors to your liking.

Pro Tips:

1. Roast multiple garlic heads at once and store the extras in an airtight container in the refrigerator for future use in various dishes.
2. To speed up the roasting process, you can use a small muffin tin to roast individual garlic heads.

Enhancing with Parmesan

Parmesan cheese is a key element in the classic Caesar dressing, but when combined with roasted garlic, it reaches new heights of flavor. In this section, we explore how the addition of Parmesan enhances the dressing, imparting a lusciousness that will leave you craving more.

Quality Matters:

opt for freshly grated Parmesan cheese to ensure the dressing is infused with the authentic and nutty flavors of this delightful cheese.

Adjusting Cheesy Goodness:

Fine-tune the amount of Parmesan to your taste preferences, ensuring it enriches the dressing without overpowering it.

Embrace the richness of roasted garlic and Parmesan, and let their enchanting flavors elevate your Caesar dressing to a new level of culinary indulgence. Savor the robust and luxurious experience as the dressing becomes a true masterpiece for your salads. Prepare to be enchanted by the caramelized goodness of roasted garlic and the velvety richness of Parmesan, creating a dressing that captivates your senses and delights your palate with each savory bite.

Chapter 11: Low-Sodium and Heart-Healthy Option

Health-Conscious Choices: Reducing Sodium

In this chapter, we explore a health-conscious twist on the classic Caesar dressing, focusing on reducing sodium content without compromising on flavor. A low-sodium and heart-healthy Caesar dressing is a great option for those looking to make more mindful choices without sacrificing taste. Discover how to lower the sodium levels in the dressing while maintaining its deliciousness, making it suitable for individuals with dietary restrictions and those seeking a more heart-friendly option.

Ingredients:

- 2 garlic cloves, minced
- 1 tablespoon Dijon mustard (choose a low-sodium option if available)
- 1/4 cup freshly squeezed lemon juice
- 1/4 cup low-sodium chicken or vegetable broth
- 1/4 cup extra-virgin olive oil
- 1 tablespoon grated Parmesan cheese (use a reduced-sodium variety, if possible)
- Salt-free seasoning blend, to taste
- Freshly ground black pepper, to taste

Instructions:

1. In a mixing bowl, combine the minced garlic and Dijon mustard, whisking them together to create a flavorful base.
2. Add the freshly squeezed lemon juice and low-sodium chicken or vegetable broth to the bowl, whisking until the flavors are well incorporated.
3. Gradually drizzle in the extra-virgin olive oil while whisking

continuously, allowing the dressing to emulsify and achieve a creamy consistency.

4. Stir in the grated Parmesan cheese, which adds a touch of richness to the dressing without contributing excessive sodium.

5. Season the dressing with a salt-free seasoning blend, adding a variety of herbs and spices to enhance the flavor without the need for additional salt.

6. Finish by seasoning with freshly ground black pepper to your liking.

Pro Tips:

1. Look for low-sodium versions of Dijon mustard, chicken or vegetable broth, and grated Parmesan cheese in your local grocery store.

2. You can also make your own salt-free seasoning blend by combining herbs such as basil, oregano, thyme, and rosemary with garlic powder and onion powder.

Substituting with Nutritious Alternatives

In this section, we explore nutritious alternatives that can replace higher-sodium ingredients, ensuring your Caesar dressing remains heart-healthy and delicious.

Low-Sodium Broth:

opt for low-sodium chicken or vegetable broth to replace regular broth without compromising the dressing's flavor and consistency.

Parmesan with a Twist:

Use a reduced-sodium or low-sodium variety of grated Parmesan cheese, which still adds a delightful umami touch to the dressing.

Salt-Free Seasoning:

Enhance the flavor profile with a salt-free seasoning blend that includes a mix of dried herbs, spices, and natural flavors.

By making these health-conscious choices and incorporating nutritious alternatives, you'll create a low-sodium and heart-healthy Caesar dressing that will satisfy your taste buds and support your well-being. Embrace the mindful approach to flavor and nutrition, as the dressing becomes a nourishing option that allows you to enjoy your favorite Caesar salads guilt-free. Prepare to savor the delightful balance of flavors, knowing that you are making a positive choice for your health with every drizzle of this heart-healthy Caesar dressing.

Chapter 12: Creamy Dijon Caesar Dressing

Dijon Mustard's Elegance in Caesar Dressing

In this chapter, we explore the elegance of Dijon mustard as it takes center stage in a creamy twist on the classic Caesar dressing. Dijon mustard brings a unique zing and sophistication to the dressing, elevating its flavor profile to new heights. Prepare to indulge in a creamy Caesar dressing that strikes a perfect balance between smooth creaminess and delightful tanginess, creating a dressing that is both luxurious and utterly delicious.

Ingredients:

- 2 garlic cloves, minced
- 2 tablespoons Dijon mustard
- 1/4 cup freshly squeezed lemon juice
- 1/2 cup mayonnaise
- 1/4 cup extra-virgin olive oil
- 1/4 cup grated Parmesan cheese
- Salt and freshly ground black pepper, to taste

Instructions:

1. In a mixing bowl, combine the minced garlic and Dijon mustard, whisking them together to create a zesty and flavorful base.
2. Add the freshly squeezed lemon juice to the bowl, whisking until the flavors meld into a harmonious combination.
3. Stir in the mayonnaise, which imparts a luscious creaminess to the dressing while amplifying the tanginess of the Dijon mustard.
4. Gradually drizzle in the extra-virgin olive oil while whisking continuously, allowing the dressing to emulsify and achieve a smooth and velvety texture.
5. Stir in the grated Parmesan cheese, which adds a rich umami flavor and a touch of indulgence to the dressing.
6. Season the dressing with salt and freshly ground black pepper, adjusting

the flavors to your liking.

Pro Tips:

1. opt for a high-quality Dijon mustard to fully appreciate its elegant and complex flavor profile in the dressing.
2. For a lighter version, use light or low-fat mayonnaise, but keep in mind that it might alter the creaminess and richness slightly.

Combining Creaminess and Zing

The creamy Dijon Caesar dressing strikes the perfect harmony between its luxurious texture and the zingy excitement of Dijon mustard. In this section, we delve into the art of combining creaminess and zing, ensuring that each element complements the other to create a dressing that dazzles the palate.

Mayonnaise Magic:

Mayonnaise brings a velvety smoothness that coats the taste buds with its creamy texture, while the tanginess of Dijon mustard adds a delightful zing that lingers.

Balancing Act:

Adjust the amount of Dijon mustard to suit your taste preferences. For a more pronounced zing, increase the quantity; for a milder tang, use a little less.

Embrace the elegance of Dijon mustard and its delightful zing as you prepare to savor the creamy Caesar dressing that awaits. Get ready to indulge in a luxurious blend of smoothness and tanginess, as this dressing becomes the epitome of sophistication for your Caesar salads. Prepare to experience a flavor journey that combines creaminess and zing in a delightful culinary dance that will delight your taste buds with every luscious mouthful.

Chapter 13: Asian-inspired Sesame Caesar Dressing

A Fusion of Flavors: Sesame and Umami

In this chapter, we embark on a culinary adventure that infuses the classic Caesar dressing with the tantalizing flavors of Asia. The fusion of nutty sesame and savory umami elements creates an unforgettable and unique taste experience. Get ready to indulge in an Asian-inspired Sesame Caesar dressing that will transport your salads to a realm of exotic flavors and harmonious blends.

Ingredients:

- 2 garlic cloves, minced
- 1 tablespoon soy sauce (low-sodium, if preferred)
- 1/4 cup rice vinegar
- 1 tablespoon toasted sesame oil
- 1 tablespoon Dijon mustard
- 1/4 cup extra-virgin olive oil
- 1 tablespoon sesame seeds, lightly toasted
- 1 teaspoon honey or maple syrup (optional, for a touch of sweetness)
- Salt and freshly ground black pepper, to taste

Instructions:

1. In a mixing bowl, combine the minced garlic and soy sauce, whisking them together to form a flavorful base with a hint of umami.
2. Add the rice vinegar and toasted sesame oil to the bowl, whisking until the dressing embraces the distinct nutty aroma of sesame.
3. Stir in the Dijon mustard, which adds a zesty kick that complements the Asian-inspired flavors.
4. Gradually drizzle in the extra-virgin olive oil while whisking continuously, allowing the dressing to emulsify and achieve a velvety texture.

5. Add the toasted sesame seeds to the dressing, enhancing it with a delightful nutty crunch.
6. For a touch of sweetness, incorporate honey or maple syrup and whisk until it's well distributed throughout the dressing.
7. Season the dressing with salt and freshly ground black pepper, adjusting the flavors to your liking.

Pro Tips:

1. Look for toasted sesame oil in Asian grocery stores or the international section of your local supermarket for a more authentic flavor.
2. To toast the sesame seeds, heat them in a dry pan over medium heat, stirring frequently until they become golden brown and fragrant.

Complementing with Asian Ingredients

The key to the success of this Asian-inspired Sesame Caesar dressing lies in the harmonious combination of Asian ingredients that complement the classic Caesar base. In this section, we explore these flavorful additions, creating a dressing that is both familiar and exotic.

Soy Sauce Magic:

Soy sauce brings the delightful umami essence to the dressing, perfectly complementing the nutty sesame and zesty Dijon mustard.

Rice Vinegar Elegance:

Rice vinegar adds a subtle tartness that enhances the dressing's flavor profile while maintaining its light and refreshing nature.

Toasted Sesame Seeds:

Toasted sesame seeds contribute a nutty crunch that elevates the dressing's texture and enhances its overall Asian flair.

Touch of Sweetness:

A hint of honey or maple syrup balances the tanginess of the dressing, offering a touch of sweetness that rounds out the flavors.

Prepare to be transported to the enchanting world of Asian-inspired flavors as you savor the delightful fusion of sesame and umami in this Caesar dressing. Embrace the exotic allure of Asia and enjoy a salad experience that harmoniously blends the best of two culinary realms. Prepare to elevate your Caesar salads with a dressing that offers an exciting and unforgettable flavor journey.

Chapter 14: Wholesome Greek Yogurt Caesar Dressing

Protein-Packed Goodness: Greek Yogurt

In this chapter, we explore the wholesome goodness of Greek yogurt as it takes center stage in a protein-packed twist on the classic Caesar dressing. Greek yogurt brings a creamy and velvety texture while infusing the dressing with a generous dose of protein. Get ready to indulge in a Caesar dressing that not only delights your taste buds but also nourishes your body with its nutritious qualities.

Ingredients:

- 1/2 cup plain Greek yogurt
- 2 garlic cloves, minced
- 1 tablespoon Dijon mustard
- 1/4 cup freshly squeezed lemon juice
- 1/4 cup extra-virgin olive oil
- 1/4 cup grated Parmesan cheese
- Salt and freshly ground black pepper, to taste

Instructions:

1. In a mixing bowl, combine the plain Greek yogurt, minced garlic, and Dijon mustard, stirring well to create a creamy and flavorful yogurt base.
2. Add the freshly squeezed lemon juice to the bowl, whisking until the flavors meld together harmoniously.
3. Gradually drizzle in the extra-virgin olive oil while continuously whisking, allowing the dressing to emulsify and achieve a smooth and velvety consistency.
4. Stir in the grated Parmesan cheese, which adds a touch of richness to the dressing without overwhelming the yogurt's creaminess.
5. Season the dressing with salt and freshly ground black pepper, adjusting the flavors to your liking.

Pro Tips:

1. Choose full-fat Greek yogurt for a creamier dressing, or opt for low-fat or non-fat yogurt for a lighter version.
2. For a vegan option, use dairy-free plain Greek yogurt made from almond, soy, or coconut milk.

Greek-Inspired Additions

Embrace the Greek inspiration and elevate your Caesar dressing with delightful additions that complement the yogurt base. In this section, we explore Greek-inspired ingredients that transform the dressing into a wholesome and vibrant culinary creation.

Kalamata Olives:

Incorporate the bold and briny flavors of Kalamata olives, adding a Mediterranean flair that pairs beautifully with Greek yogurt.

Cucumber Freshness:

Add a refreshing crunch with diced cucumber, lending a cool and hydrating element to your Caesar dressing.

Red Onion Allure:

Introduce thinly sliced red onion for a touch of sharpness and vibrant color, creating a delightful visual appeal.

Fresh Dill Delight:

Embrace the herbaceous charm of fresh dill, which enhances the dressing with a zesty and citrusy note.

Prepare to relish the protein-packed goodness of Greek yogurt in this wholesome Caesar dressing. Embrace the Mediterranean-inspired additions and enjoy a salad experience that nourishes your body and delights your palate. Get ready to elevate your Caesar salads with a dressing that combines creamy yogurt and tantalizing Greek flavors, creating a wholesome and nutritious feast for your senses.

Chapter 15: Pesto Caesar Dressing

Italian Fusion: The Marriage of Pesto and Caesar

In this chapter, we celebrate the harmonious union of two Italian culinary favorites—the classic Caesar dressing and the vibrant pesto sauce. The result is a delightful Pesto Caesar dressing that brings together the best of both worlds. Prepare to indulge in a fusion of flavors that marries the creaminess of Caesar with the nutty and herbal elements of pesto, creating a dressing that is rich, aromatic, and undeniably irresistible.

Ingredients:

- 2 garlic cloves, minced
- 1/4 cup freshly squeezed lemon juice
- 1 tablespoon Dijon mustard
- 1/4 cup grated Parmesan cheese
- 1/4 cup pine nuts or walnuts, toasted
- 1 cup fresh basil leaves
- 1/4 cup extra-virgin olive oil
- Salt and freshly ground black pepper, to taste

Instructions:

1. In a food processor or blender, combine the minced garlic and freshly squeezed lemon juice, blending until they form a zesty and flavorful base.
2. Add the Dijon mustard and grated Parmesan cheese to the processor or blender, continuing to blend until the flavors meld together beautifully.
3. Incorporate the toasted pine nuts or walnuts into the mixture, adding the delightful nutty element that characterizes pesto.
4. Add the fresh basil leaves to the food processor or blender, blending until the dressing embraces the aromatic essence of the herb.
5. Gradually drizzle in the extra-virgin olive oil while the processor or blender is running on low speed, allowing the dressing to emulsify and

achieve a velvety consistency.

6. Season the dressing with salt and freshly ground black pepper, adjusting the flavors to your liking.

Pro Tips:

1. To toast the pine nuts or walnuts, simply heat them in a dry pan over medium heat, stirring frequently until they become golden brown and fragrant.
2. For a more pronounced herbal flavor, add a splash of pesto sauce to the dressing.

Nutty and Herbal Elements

The magic of this Pesto Caesar dressing lies in the nutty and herbal elements that blend seamlessly, creating an Italian fusion that delights the senses. In this section, we explore the key ingredients that infuse the dressing with its irresistible charm.

Toasted Pine Nuts or Walnuts:

Toasted pine nuts or walnuts lend a delightful nutty crunch to the dressing, adding depth and complexity to the flavor profile.

Fresh Basil Leaves:

Fresh basil is the heart of pesto and brings an aromatic and herbal freshness to the dressing, elevating its character.

Aromatic Garlic:

The minced garlic infuses the dressing with a zesty kick, balancing the creaminess and herbal notes with its pungent essence.

Prepare to savor the culinary marvel that is the Pesto Caesar dressing—a fusion of Italian flavors that will transport your salads to the sunny hillsides of Italy. Embrace the nutty and herbal elements as they weave together, creating a dressing that is both comforting and exotic. Get ready to elevate your Caesar salads with a Pesto Caesar dressing that is the epitome of Italian fusion and culinary delight.

Chapter 16: Sweet and Savory Honey Mustard Caesar Dressing

Sweet and Tangy Notes of Honey Mustard

In this chapter, we explore a delectable combination of sweet and savory flavors with the marriage of honey mustard and the classic Caesar dressing. The resulting Sweet and Savory Honey Mustard Caesar dressing offers a delightful medley of taste sensations that will captivate your palate. Get ready to indulge in a dressing that balances the sweetness of honey with the tanginess of mustard, creating a symphony of flavors that will elevate your Caesar salads to a whole new level.

Ingredients:

- 2 garlic cloves, minced
- 1 tablespoon Dijon mustard
- 2 tablespoons honey
- 1/4 cup freshly squeezed lemon juice
- 1/4 cup extra-virgin olive oil
- 1/4 cup grated Parmesan cheese
- Salt and freshly ground black pepper, to taste

Instructions:

1. In a mixing bowl, combine the minced garlic, Dijon mustard, and honey, stirring well to create a sweet and tangy base.
2. Add the freshly squeezed lemon juice to the bowl, whisking until the flavors meld together harmoniously.
3. Gradually drizzle in the extra-virgin olive oil while whisking continuously, allowing the dressing to emulsify and achieve a smooth and velvety consistency.
4. Stir in the grated Parmesan cheese, which adds a touch of richness to the dressing without overpowering the sweet and tangy notes of honey mustard.
5. Season the dressing with salt and freshly ground black pepper, adjusting the flavors to your liking.

Pro Tips:

1. Experiment with different types of honey to find the one that suits your taste preferences best. From floral to fruity, each variety offers unique nuances to the dressing.
2. For a creamier texture, you can also add a dollop of mayonnaise or Greek yogurt to the dressing.

Balancing Sweetness with Other Flavors

The key to a successful Sweet and Savory Honey Mustard Caesar dressing lies in finding the perfect balance between sweetness and other flavors. In this section, we explore the art of balancing the sweet and tangy notes to create a harmonious and delightful dressing.

Honey's Delicate Sweetness:

Honey brings a gentle and natural sweetness to the dressing, which complements the tanginess of the mustard and lemon juice.

Dijon Mustard's Piquant Tang:

Dijon mustard adds a zesty kick that harmonizes beautifully with the sweetness of honey, offering a delightful contrast of flavors.

Acidity of Lemon Juice:

Freshly squeezed lemon juice provides a bright and citrusy punch, enhancing the overall balance of the dressing.

Prepare to savor the delightful medley of sweet and savory notes in this Honey Mustard Caesar dressing—a dressing that tantalizes your taste buds and leaves you craving more. Embrace the delightful interplay of flavors as the sweetness of honey and the tanginess of mustard dance together in perfect harmony. Get ready to elevate your Caesar salads with a dressing that offers a delightful symphony of taste sensations—a dressing that will surely become a favorite on your dining table.

Chapter 17: Roasted Red Pepper Caesar Dressing

Bold and Colorful: Roasted Red Pepper

In this chapter, we embark on a culinary journey that celebrates the bold and colorful flavors of roasted red pepper as it transforms the classic Caesar dressing. The addition of roasted red pepper brings a delightful smokiness and a burst of vibrant color to the dressing, elevating it to new heights of taste and visual appeal. Get ready to indulge in a Roasted Red Pepper Caesar dressing that is both bold and beautiful, capturing the essence of roasted pepper perfection.

Ingredients:

- 1 large red bell pepper
- 2 garlic cloves, minced
- 1 tablespoon Dijon mustard
- 1/4 cup freshly squeezed lemon juice
- 1/4 cup extra-virgin olive oil
- 1/4 cup grated Parmesan cheese
- Salt and freshly ground black pepper, to taste

Instructions:

1. Preheat your oven to 400°F (200°C).
2. Place the red bell pepper on a baking sheet lined with aluminum foil.
3. Roast the red bell pepper in the preheated oven for 20-25 minutes, turning it occasionally, until the skin is charred and blistered.
4. Remove the pepper from the oven and transfer it to a bowl. Cover the bowl with plastic wrap and let it sit for 10 minutes. This will steam the pepper, making it easier to peel.
5. After 10 minutes, peel off the skin of the red pepper and remove the stem and seeds. Slice the pepper into small pieces.
6. In a mixing bowl, combine the minced garlic, Dijon mustard, and the

sliced roasted red pepper, stirring well to create a smoky and flavorful base.

7. Add the freshly squeezed lemon juice to the bowl, whisking until the flavors meld together beautifully.

8. Gradually drizzle in the extra-virgin olive oil while whisking continuously, allowing the dressing to emulsify and achieve a velvety consistency.

9. Stir in the grated Parmesan cheese, which adds a touch of richness to the dressing without overpowering the roasted red pepper's smoky essence.

10. Season the dressing with salt and freshly ground black pepper, adjusting the flavors to your liking.

Pro Tips:

To roast the red bell pepper on an open flame, use tongs to hold the pepper over a gas stove burner. Rotate the pepper until all sides are charred, then proceed with steaming and peeling as described.

A Pepper Profile

The star of this Roasted Red Pepper Caesar dressing is, of course, the roasted red pepper itself. In this section, we delve into the profile of this bold and colorful ingredient, understanding how it contributes to the dressing's taste and visual appeal.

Smoky Perfection:

Roasting the red bell pepper imparts a smoky essence that enhances the dressing with depth and complexity.

Vibrant Visual Appeal:

The vibrant red color of the roasted pepper brightens up the dressing, adding a pop of color to your Caesar salads.

Prepare to savor the bold and colorful flavors of the Roasted Red Pepper Caesar dressing—a dressing that captivates your senses and elevates your salads to a feast for the eyes and palate. Embrace the smoky perfection of roasted red pepper as it weaves its magic into the classic Caesar dressing. Get ready for a taste experience that is both bold and beautiful, leaving you utterly enchanted with each savory drizzle of this Roasted Red Pepper Caesar dressing.

Chapter 18: Tahini Caesar Dressing

Nutty and Creamy: Incorporating Tahini

In this chapter, we explore the rich and creamy world of tahini as it becomes the star ingredient in a unique twist on the classic Caesar dressing. Tahini, a paste made from ground sesame seeds, brings a delightful nutty flavor and velvety texture to the dressing, elevating it to new heights of taste and creaminess. Get ready to indulge in a Tahini Caesar dressing that is both luscious and exotic, infusing your salads with a Middle Eastern flair.

Ingredients:

- 2 garlic cloves, minced
- 2 tablespoons tahini
- 1 tablespoon Dijon mustard
- 1/4 cup freshly squeezed lemon juice
- 1/4 cup extra-virgin olive oil
- 1/4 cup grated Parmesan cheese
- Salt and freshly ground black pepper, to taste

Instructions:

1. In a mixing bowl, combine the minced garlic, tahini, and Dijon mustard, stirring well to create a nutty and creamy tahini base.
2. Add the freshly squeezed lemon juice to the bowl, whisking until the flavors meld together harmoniously.
3. Gradually drizzle in the extra-virgin olive oil while whisking continuously, allowing the dressing to emulsify and achieve a smooth and velvety consistency.
4. Stir in the grated Parmesan cheese, which adds a touch of richness to the dressing without overwhelming the nutty essence of tahini.
5. Season the dressing with salt and freshly ground black pepper, adjusting the flavors to your liking.

Pro Tips:

1. Use high-quality tahini for the best results, as it will have a smooth and rich texture with a more pronounced nutty flavor.
2. Tahini can naturally separate, so be sure to stir it well before measuring and incorporating it into the dressing.

Working with Middle Eastern Flavors

Tahini introduces Middle Eastern flavors to the classic Caesar dressing, creating a culinary fusion that tantalizes the taste buds. In this section, we explore the art of working with these exotic flavors, ensuring a harmonious balance that celebrates the allure of tahini.

Nutty Goodness of Tahini:

Tahini brings a delightful nutty flavor to the dressing, which complements the creamy and savory nature of the classic Caesar base.

Embracing Middle Eastern Elements:

The combination of tahini with Dijon mustard and lemon juice adds a hint of zing that harmonizes beautifully with the Middle Eastern flair.

Prepare to savor the rich and creamy delights of the Tahini Caesar dressing—a dressing that infuses your salads with an exotic Middle Eastern twist. Embrace the lusciousness of tahini and the allure of Middle Eastern flavors as they dance together in perfect harmony. Get ready to elevate your Caesar salads with a dressing that is both nutty and creamy—a dressing that will whisk your taste buds away on a journey to the enchanting realm of the Middle East.

Chapter 19: Whiskey-Glazed Caesar Dressing

Spirited Dressing: Whiskey's Warmth

In this chapter, we delve into the world of spirits as we introduce the warm and distinctive flavors of whiskey into the classic Caesar dressing. The addition of whiskey brings a spirited twist to the dressing, infusing it with rich and complex notes that add depth and warmth to every bite. Get ready to indulge in a Whiskey-Glazed Caesar dressing that is both bold and refined, elevating your salads with a touch of sophistication.

Ingredients:

- 2 garlic cloves, minced
- 1 tablespoon Dijon mustard
- 1/4 cup whiskey (bourbon or your preferred whiskey)
- 1/4 cup freshly squeezed lemon juice
- 1/4 cup extra-virgin olive oil
- 1/4 cup grated Parmesan cheese
- Salt and freshly ground black pepper, to taste

Instructions:

1. In a mixing bowl, combine the minced garlic and Dijon mustard, stirring well to create a zesty and flavorful base.
2. Add the whiskey to the bowl, whisking until the spirit's warmth melds beautifully with the dressing.
3. Pour in the freshly squeezed lemon juice, whisking to balance the dressing's richness with a bright and citrusy punch.
4. Gradually drizzle in the extra-virgin olive oil while whisking continuously, allowing the dressing to emulsify and achieve a velvety texture.
5. Stir in the grated Parmesan cheese, which adds a touch of richness to the dressing without overpowering the whiskey's unique character.
6. Season the dressing with salt and freshly ground black pepper, adjusting

the flavors to your liking.

Pro Tips:

1. Choose a whiskey that you enjoy, as its flavor will be pronounced in the dressing. Bourbon or other whiskey varieties with warm and slightly sweet notes work well in this recipe.
2. For a smokier version, consider using a peated whiskey, which will add a distinctive smoky undertone to the dressing.

Pairing with Different Greens

The bold and spirited Whiskey-Glazed Caesar dressing complements various greens, making it a versatile choice for your salads. In this section, we explore different greens that harmonize beautifully with this spirited dressing.

Crisp Romaine Lettuce:

The classic choice for a Caesar salad, romaine lettuce's crunch pairs splendidly with the robust flavors of the Whiskey-Glazed dressing.

Lively Arugula:

The peppery and slightly bitter notes of arugula balance wonderfully with the warmth of the whiskey, creating a vibrant and lively combination.

Hearty Kale:

Kale's sturdy leaves provide a hearty base for the dressing, allowing its deep flavors to shine through.

Mixed Baby Greens:

A mix of baby greens offers a delightful variety of textures and flavors, harmonizing well with the complexity of the Whiskey-Glazed dressing.

Prepare to savor the spirited delight of the Whiskey-Glazed Caesar dressing—a dressing that adds warmth and depth to your salads. Embrace the boldness of whiskey as it brings a touch of sophistication to the classic Caesar dressing. Get ready to elevate your salads with a dressing that is both spirited and refined—a dressing that will undoubtedly leave a lasting impression on your taste buds and elevate your dining experience to a whole new level.

Chapter 20: Serving and Storing Tips

Perfect Presentation: Plating Ideas

In this final chapter, we explore the art of presenting your homemade Caesar dressings in a way that not only tantalizes the taste buds but also delights the eyes. The perfect presentation enhances the dining experience, making your salads even more inviting and memorable. Here are some plating ideas to elevate your Caesar salads to the next level:

Classic Caesar Salad: Toss crisp romaine lettuce with the Classic Caesar dressing, then garnish with shaved Parmesan cheese, croutons, and a sprinkle of freshly ground black pepper.

Mediterranean Twist: Drizzle the Mediterranean Caesar dressing over a mix of romaine lettuce, Kalamata olives, cherry tomatoes, feta cheese, and fresh oregano leaves for a taste of the Mediterranean.

Creamy Avocado Delight: Serve the Creamy Avocado Caesar dressing with a bed of mixed baby greens, cherry tomatoes, avocado slices, and toasted pumpkin seeds for a creamy and nutritious delight.

Spicy Caesar Kick: Toss spicy arugula with the Spicy Caesar dressing, then top with grilled chicken strips, sliced jalapeños, and a sprinkle of crushed red pepper flakes.

Low-Sodium Heart-Healthy Option: For the health-conscious, serve the Low-Sodium and Heart-Healthy Caesar dressing with kale, cherry tomatoes, cucumbers, and grilled shrimp for a guilt-free indulgence.

Keeping It Fresh: Storing Your Homemade Dressings

Proper storage is essential to maintain the quality and freshness of your homemade Caesar dressings. Here are some tips on how to store your dressings to ensure they remain flavorful and delicious:

Refrigeration: Store all the dressings in airtight containers or jars and refrigerate them promptly after preparation. This will help preserve their taste and prevent spoilage.

Labeling: Remember to label each container with the name of the dressing and the date it was made. This ensures you can easily identify and use the dressings within their recommended storage period.

Shelf Life: Most homemade Caesar dressings can be stored in the refrigerator for up to one week. Creamy dressings may have a shorter shelf life, so consume them within 3-5 days.

Separation: It's normal for some dressings to separate over time. Before using, give the dressing a good stir or shake to recombine the ingredients.

Freezing (Non-Creamy Dressings): If you have a surplus of non-creamy dressings, you can freeze them in small portions for up to three months. Thaw them in the refrigerator before use.

Avoid Freezing Creamy Dressings: Creamy dressings do not freeze well due to the potential for texture changes. It's best to make creamy dressings in smaller batches to avoid wastage.

By following these serving and storing tips, you'll be able to enjoy your homemade Caesar dressings to the fullest. Whether you're serving them for a casual family meal or a special dinner party, the perfect presentation and proper storage will ensure that each salad is a delicious and memorable experience for everyone at the table.

Congratulations on completing this cookbook journey! Your creativity and adventurous spirit in exploring different Caesar dressing variations will undoubtedly inspire many to create their own culinary masterpieces. May your salads always be dressed to perfection and may your dining experiences be filled with joy and satisfaction! Happy cooking and bon appétit!

In this cookbook, we embarked on a flavorful and creative journey into the world of Caesar salad dressings. We explored the classic Caesar dressing, its rich history, and essential ingredients. From there, we ventured into an array of delightful variations, each bringing its own unique twist to the traditional recipe.

We dived into the realms of avocado, lemon, garlic, anchovies, and even chipotle, uncovering the secrets of balancing flavors and customizing spice levels. The Mediterranean-inspired dressings took us on a culinary trip to sun-kissed lands, while the yogurt-based and low-sodium options catered to health-conscious tastes. Our exploration didn't stop there—Dijon mustard, Asian-inspired sesame, roasted garlic, and whiskey-glazed dressings added new dimensions to our Caesar creations.

Tahini introduced us to Middle Eastern delights, while honey mustard and pesto brought sweet and herbal elements into the mix. The roasted red pepper dressing not only delighted with its vibrant color but also embraced a smoky allure.

Finally, we explored the art of perfect presentation, offering various plating ideas to enhance the visual appeal of our Caesar salads. We also learned the importance of proper storage to keep our homemade dressings fresh and flavorful.

With each chapter, we celebrated the beauty of culinary experimentation, encouraging you to create and customize dressings according to your taste preferences and culinary adventures. The joy of cooking lies in embracing creativity, exploring new flavors, and making each meal a delightful experience.

As we conclude this cookbook, may your culinary journey continue to be filled with delicious discoveries and delightful creations. Whether you're preparing a simple weekday salad or hosting a special dinner, these Caesar dressings are here to elevate your salads and bring joy to your table.

Thank you for joining us on this flavorful adventure. Happy cooking, and may your salads always be dressed with love, passion, and the joy of exploring the art of dressing! Bon appétit!

www.ingramcontent.com/pod-product-compliance
Lightning Source LLC
Chambersburg PA
CBHW070316160726
47999CB00003B/1045